"BE CAREFUL!"

CREDITS

Producer
Ron Berry

Editor
Orly Kelly

What to do
when your mom or dad says ...

"BE CAREFUL!"

By
JOY BERRY

GROLIER ENTERPRISES CORP.

Has your mother or father ever told you to . . .

When your parents tell you to be careful, do you wonder. . .

If this sounds familiar to you, you're going to **love** this book.

Because this book is going to tell you exactly how to be careful.

SAFETY AT HOME

Be Careful with Electricity

You can prevent electrical shocks if you take certain precautions.

Do not drape an electric cord across a heater, bathtub or sink.

Do not stretch an electric cord across an area where people must walk.

Do not turn an electrical switch on or off, or plug a cord into the socket, with wet hands or while standing on a wet floor.

Do not plug more than two appliances into a double wall socket.

If an appliance blows a fuse when you turn it on or plug it in, unplug it immediately.

Do not probe appliances with a metal knife, fork or other instrument while they are plugged in.

Always unplug appliances before cleaning or adjusting them and after you have finished using them.

Pull plugs from the sockets by the plug only, not by the cord.

Be Careful with Gas

You can prevent explosion and/or the inhalation of toxic fumes if you—

* turn a gas appliance off if a flame does not appear 3 to 5 seconds after turning it on, and

- notify an adult immediately if you smell gas fumes.

Be Careful with Fire

You can prevent fires if you—

- do not play with matches or lighters, and

- notify an adult immediately if you see anything that could possibly start a fire.

Fires are often caused by—

- unattended lighted cigarettes

- defective heating equipment

- too many plugs in one socket

- frayed or taped wires

- combustible materials left or stored too close to an open flame

- careless storage of cleaning products or fuel (petroleum products).

15

Be Careful with Heat

You can prevent burns if you—

- do not touch anything when it is hot (such as a stove or heater), and

- use mittens or potholders when you handle anything that is hot.

16

When cooking, always turn pot handles toward the center of the stove. This will prevent anyone from accidentally knocking the pot off the stove.

Be Careful with Water

You can prevent burns if you—

- adjust the water temperature before stepping into a tub or shower, and

- check the temperature before you immerse your hands in hot water such as water running from the tap or dishwater.

You can prevent falls if you—

- use a rubber mat when bathing or showering or place decorative, nonskid decals on the floor of the bathtub or shower,

- pick up soap bars and soap pieces from the tub and floor,

- rinse out the tub after use to remove slippery soap film, and

- wipe up a wet floor.

19

Be Careful with Medications

You can be sure that you do not take too much, or the wrong kind of, medication if you—

- do not take medicine of any kind without adult supervision.

It is best if you—

- do not take medicines which have been prescribed for someone else,

- do not take medicines in the dark, and

- check the label before taking any medicine.

21

Be Careful with Clutter

You can prevent accidents if you—

- remove toys and equipment from floors, stairs, walkways and driveways,

- keep walkways and steps free of ice and wet leaves, and

- remove all broken glass and rubbish in and around the house.

Be Careful with Steps, Stairs and Ladders

You can prevent falls if you—

- use only well-lighted steps and stairs, and

- use a sturdy support, like a step stool or ladder, when reaching up to high places.

23

Be Careful with Dangerous Things

Do not use any of the following items without adult supervision:

- aerosol and spray cans
- chemicals
- knives and other sharp kitchen utensils
- razors
- dangerous recreational equipment
- electrical appliances
- tools
- matches or cigarette lighters
- explosives or fireworks
- guns

Also, do not play in or around a vehicle (such as a car or truck).

SAFETY AT SCHOOL

Be Careful on the Way To and From School

When you leave for school, go directly to the school. When you leave for home, go directly home. Do not stop along the way. Do not use a different than usual route, unless your family or the school knows of your plans.

Be Careful at School

To insure your safety and the safety of others, your school has established rules. There are rules for—

• indoor areas (such as the classroom and the cafeteria),

• outdoor areas (such as the playground and parking lot),

• outings and special events, and

• emergency procedures.

It is important for you to know what these rules are and to cooperate with them completely.

SAFETY IN THE COMMUNITY

Be Careful When You Are a Pedestrian

Wear light-colored or reflective clothing when you walk in the dark so that drivers can see you.

Watch for vehicles in driveway, alleys and parking lots. Before you walk behind a vehicle, be sure it is not moving.

Always be alert and be prepared to stop. Never rely on anyone else to see you.

28

Do not accept a ride from a stranger.

Choose the safest route when planning your walk. A safe route is one with sidewalks, traffic signals and marked crosswalks. If there is no sidewalk, walk facing the traffic.

31

Look both ways before crossing a street. When you are certain that no vehicle is coming, *walk*—don't run—across the street.

Cross the street at an intersection where drivers expect to see pedestrians.

Use crosswalks whenever possible.

On a street with several lanes, cross one lane at a time. Make sure that the traffic in each lane stops for you before you proceed.

33

A pedestrian signal changes from "Walk" to "Don't Walk." When the signal says "Walk," you may cross the street if there are no vehicles coming.

If there is a traffic signal instead of a pedestrian signal, cross the street when the light turns green. Be sure that there are no vehicles coming before you proceed.

At intersections without signals, wait for the vehicles to stop before you cross the street.

Do not try to make vehicles stop for you by stepping into the street in front of them.

Make sure drivers see you. Do not walk in front of a vehicle until you see the driver looking at you.

Be Careful When You Are Riding a Bike

You can prevent accidents if you—

- learn how to ride your bicycle with skill and coordination, and

- practice riding in safe places, such as

   your own yard

   your driveway

   a playground (when it is not crowded)

   a street that is closed to traffic.

Keep your bicycle in good condition.

Make sure that your bicycle is equipped with a light and an appropriate number of reflectors, if you plan to ride it in the dark.

Do not ride your bike in heavy rains or snow, or when the roads are icy.

Wear light-colored or reflective clothing when riding in the dark.

Do not hitch rides on moving vehicles.

Do not carry passengers on your bike. Put all parcels, books or packages in the basket or rack.

Keep your eyes directed to the road and be ready
for emergencies. Always ride on the right side of
the street. Always give pedestrians and motor
vehicles the right of way.

Obey all traffic signs and signals.

Always use proper hand signals to let others know what you intend to do.

When crossing streets, proceed as you would if you were a pedestrian. Look both ways, cross at intersections and use crosswalks.

Walk your bike across busy streets and intersections.

Never ride out into the street from between parked cars, or from alleys or driveways, without stopping to look for oncoming vehicles.

Never weave in and out of traffic.

Never pass a bike or other vehicle on a hill, curve or intersection.

Ride in single file when riding in a group.

Be Careful When You Are a Passenger

You can prevent accidents if you—

- do not distract the driver of a car or bus by talking too loudly or being too active,

- do not put your head or arms out of the window of a moving vehicle, and

- always wear your seat belt when riding in a car.

Be Careful Around Dangerous Places

Be careful in and around dangerous areas. It is best to have an adult accompany and supervise you when you are in these places:

animal trails
caves
driveways and parking lots
high places
places where large machines are stored
unexplored, uninhabited areas
streets and highways
bodies of water

SAFETY WHILE ON VACATION

Be Careful When You Are Swimming

You can avoid a swimming or diving accident if you—

- learn to swim well as soon as possible,

- if you are a nonswimmer, do not rely on a safety device to keep you afloat in deep water,

- make sure that an adult who swims, or a lifeguard, is around whenever you swim,

- know how deep the water is before you dive into it,

- be careful when swimming in lakes, rivers or oceans. Current, uneven depths, surf and submerged rocks require special swimming skills and extra caution,

- always have another person with you whenever you go swimming.

Be Careful When You Are Camping and Hiking

Learn the rules and regulations that have been established for the area in which you are camping or hiking, then cooperate with the rules completely.

Do not explore the area without a guide.

Do not wander off by yourself.

Learn to identify and avoid poisonous plants, dangerous insects and other dangerous animals.

47

THE END of your mom or dad having to say, **"BE CAREFUL!"**